# BETWEEN THE VERSES AND THE INK

*Volume One*

COLLECTED POEMS BY

# BRAEDEN MICHAELS

Raw Earth Ink

2023

First paperback edition April 2023

Interior design by tara caribou

ISBN 978-1-960991-01-0 (paperback)

Published by Raw Earth Ink
PO Box 39332
Ninilchik, AK 99639
www.raw-earth-ink.com

# Table of Contents

# THE RAVEN'S POISON

"Imbibe in the rainbow of emotions."

# The Ballerina in the Snow Globe

She dances like a ballerina in a snow globe
Dandelions are adding
lyrics to the sound of Mozart

The splashes of watercolors were hanging above her elegance
She glides for forgiveness
and sways for sobriety

The tinsel around her fury spirit is no longer sparkling
She is twirling and spinning for a numb audience
The atmosphere is toxic

The ambiance in the snow globe is desolate
At the end of the ballet only one rose was thrown
in front of her feet

God threw it with all his might
Her tears fell to the floor like a tidal wave
She only needed to dance for herself

# Ceramic Villains

Stomach acid
gorges the frame of the picture
Ceramic villains
stand in the center of the image
Credit card smiles
seek the light of the troubled road
Wallets become empty
as they cling to the objects of the rooms

Love was just a word to deceive

Camouflaged tears
reckon within the twitching of souls
Charades is not
just the game
but the poison
they drink daily
They laid drunk
in the center of the bed
photographing plastic memories

Love was just a word they wanted to believe

# A Crack in the Lullaby

And the chimes on the porch
whistle to the roar
And the faucet drips a lonely
drop of sorrow into the sink

And the stairs have a thin
board to make a crying melody
And the fools in the bed
sleep beside plastic hearts

And the rusty garbage can
rattles off anticlimactic jokes
And the couch has been
reminiscing of the teenage years

And the doorknobs in the hall
sob from the ageless slams
And the coffee cups fight
over glazed donuts and cinnamon toast

And the glasses of water
seek optimism in the dark
And the comic books
in the dresser drawer salivate next
to the X Rated magazines

And the mobile in the crib
has a crack in the lullaby
And the lock on the door plays
the piano to emptiness

# Tragic Painting

Crawl inside the decorated masterpiece
Crawl in the garden of this hollow fairytale
Crawl in the trenches to gasp for air

Crawl inside this lost graveyard
Crawl inside this wound of romance
Crawl in the river between anger and hate

Crawl in the carnival to laugh at despair
Crawl inside this forgotten casket
Crawl inside this broken melody

Crawl in the words of this pale chapter
Crawl in the tainted memories
Crawl inside this tragedy without a trace

# The Raven's Poison

Once upon a midnight fear
she took a sip of corrosion
Debilitating mannerisms and quirks
fumbling through a frenzy
Gliding inside hallucinations
staggering outside the commotions
A recollection of mourning

Stern exchanges melting
comments and remarks growl
Sentiments dressed in black
treasures whispering hush
ripping dead skin with caution
crumbling faith turns into dirt
A recollection of mourning

Hunger flexing with animosity
Greed pointing with saliva
In holy matrimony with the raven
She tasted the hollow bitterness
Numb and disgusted by the poison
Infuriated with the toxic rants
A recollection of mourning

Provoked by exasperation
Anxiety wrapped around her neck
Choking on sour corruption
Addicted to the murmurs
Inhaling by a malicious tongue
A recollection of mourning

A catastrophic touch bellowed
Infatuation hung as a disaster
Benevolence was a chewed-up dog bone
Loneliness exhaled rapidly
Sympathy was an old rag
Love was just mucus from a cough
A recollection of mourning

# Rattlesnake Postcard

A restless strawberry blonde
is posing for a pickup line
The lipstick reeked desperate
measures to fill an empty void
The nicotine is vile
as the band is warming up
by playing the Allman Brothers

Charlie stumbles in through the door
cursing his ex-wife's name
The bartender chuckles
as he is pouring shots of Jack Daniels for
the bachelor partying in the corner
The conversations feel dyslexic
as the customers become trashed and plastered

Some are trying to find the answers
at the bottom of a glass
Some are trying to celebrate a victory
milestone or wash away the hollow shell
Amanda never talks to strangers
unless she has a beer in her hand
Jackson is patiently waiting
to make a transaction with Charlie

This is the place or a midnight rendezvous
The kegs are slowly disappearing
The bottles are empty just like the customers
that walk into the "Rattlesnake"
I was just reading the postcard
from Charlie and things haven't change

# Under a Bloodshot Moon

Between the blackouts and the vertigo
Slurred discussions evaporate in the smog
Excuses and cursed words creep in
Empty words reside at the bottom

Even the bloodshot moon cries

Between the collision and the stars
Sound of the gin on the rocks washes away
Sarcasm and coughed up memories
Acceptance of losses linger in the cold

Even the bloodshot moon cries

Between the anger and the doubt
Brick walls rise inside my head
Drowning in the misery and sadness
Reveling in the toxic moment

Even the bloodshot moon cries

Between the strangers and ignorance
Conversations vibrate and tremble
Loneliness staggers among the silence
Bottled up screams whisper

Even the bloodshot moon cries

# Bottle of Shadows

Leave me a pile of scrutiny
Leave me a bag of aggravation
And I will toss it in the dying closet

Leave me a tiny bit of solitude
Leave me an ounce of spoiled milk
And I will throw it in the empty pantry

Leave me a gallon of spiked juice
Leave me a shred of laughter
And I will painfully swallow the bits

Leave me a bottle of shadows
Leave me a jug of sarcasm
And I will watch myself drown

Leave me a tank of affliction
Leave me a plate of dirty lies
And I will break another mirror

Leave me a pair of worn-out glasses
Leave me a little bit of rust
And I will never see my heart ache

# Scent of Emptiness

Pulled heart strings
Recorded whispers at a dead-end street
Telephone wires ripped
And Velcro tattered wings fall

Lashing of a dangerous tongue
Transfusions of vertigo
Neon needles lit on the graveyard shift
And deafening beats of solitude cry

Pockets full of copper
Choking scrambled poison
Trails of blood money at my feet
And the silver spoon cracks

Convicted of breaking veins
Stealing the scent of perfume
Intimidating romance
And I raise the glass to loneliness

Dressed for traveler's checks
Leaving for cards and dice
Guzzling a cup of burgundy
And I toast to the shell of myself

# Rattle in a Cage

Indecisions hide like bats in the echoes of the cave
Uncertainty sips from the acidic river
Vinegar seeping between the crushed bones and sharp nerves

Isolation and desolation are thumbs ripped from each hand
And the rattle lingers in the corner of the ear drum
Dismay is tucked away behind a faded curtain

Flaws stick to me like starving fleas
Substance is the saliva dripping from the piranha's teeth
The equilibrium inside me wakes up the storm

And the rattle parades in a rhythm that disturbs the haze
Symptoms of a nontransparent disease spread
Inside the soliloquy the cage embraces the thunder

Murmurs and grumbles tremble with fright
Theology and myths walking in unison
And the rattle pounds like a headache

Butchered insults and splinters drive three inches through my anger
Crude laughs and vicious skies open up pouring sadness
Exasperation drags my eyelids through the dirt

Sorrow is a creek that I cleanse the silence
And the rattle pierces my aching skin
And I lay here with the rattle in the cage soothing the emptiness

# Cursed Diamond

Sulking in the leather booth
She sips on her vodka on the rocks
The mascara is running due to her kaleidoscope tears

She is staring down at her notepad
drawing hearts around the deceased name
Often, she struggles displaying emotions and genuine affection

She was born to be a stone
The melancholy around her knife shaped soul
swarms the emptiness

She looks at herself as if she is a cursed diamond
She is surrounded by greed, politicians, clowns, and thieves
Excuse me, aren't they all the same thing?

The wealth she accumulated over the years were other's
misfortunes
She has worn the best fake smile as the years have faded

She has aged gracefully but her withered heart has been in a life
size pinball machine

As she has sat there staring at the notepad the reality
shook her foundation

She will leave this earth without her possessions
The smoke in the air continues to thicken

# The Skeleton's Magic

From the marrow
of your bleached bones
I gawk at your cloudy view

From the vessels
of your decaying brain
I peek at your vile lungs

From the ivory skin
to your numb heart
I overlook your flaws

From the incubus
of your wretched soul
I gaze into your core

From the veins
of your savage truth
to your circus tales

I scan the turbulence
of your existence
I rejoice in seeing
the skeleton's magic

# A Smeared Overture

A smudge of fear hangs above the black eye
She discounted the punch line

A dash in the wind smacked me hard
She smeared my name in the mud

A dispersed glimpse of the breeze fades
She persecuted me based on herself

A symphony played her shattered melody
She wore a discolored gown to the palace

A blistering sky laughed at her overture
She minimized the melody within me

A belittling spirit flown around me like a fly
She plastered her arrogance in my face

A prologue was written in her cold blood
She left the epilogue before the cynicism danced

# Unspoken Dance

Sipping on brandy
As the conversations stir like drinks
In the corner of my eye
walks a stunning beauty

Candlelit piano played with only fingertips
Glancing at her crimson dress from a distance
Nonchalantly photographing her candy lips
Thoughts of caressing her skin
flow like a river through my mind

The Mayfield jazz club oozes sensuality
dripping magic and chills of the spine
Our eyes meet for the first time
and the moment stood still

The piano is playing endlessly
as I pay the check in the clouds of smoke
The dance floor is empty as I stand in the center

Volts of passion soar through my body
waiting to just dance with the most beautiful
woman in the room
Elegance walks towards me as my hands wait

I place my hands on her waist and
feel the silk of the dress
Our lips are inches
apart waiting to connect

We move to the sound of the delicate piano
and we do not speak a word

As the jazz club empties invincible fire is burning
as we continue the unspoken dance
The radiance of her beauty is astonishing

I craved her essence and warmth
I respected and cherished every second
Instead of kissing her lips
I leaned in to place my lips on her cheek

As our bodies became closer
to the sound of the piano
I whispered in her ear
"I want to make love to you."

# Sugar Fascination

I've undressed your kindness
and taste the sweet tea
I've undressed your words
and swallow your charm

I've undressed your candor
and step into your confidence
I've undressed your intellect
and fell in love with your wit

I've undressed your beliefs
and sleep with your poetry
I've undressed your receptiveness
and dance with your fire

I've undressed your sharpness
and licked your bitterness
I've undressed your magnetism
and latch on to your spell

I've undressed your enchanted eyes
and grip your mysterious soul
I've undressed your broken star
and see a magnificent galaxy

# Saturated Desire

I remember
when I felt your hunger
I can remember
when I felt your innocence

I remember
when I was saturated by your desire
I can remember
when I was embracing your touch

I remember
using that word love emphatically
I can remember
the dreams we shared

I remember
when the kiss made us cry
I can remember
when you were thirsty for me

I remember
being in a trance from the echoes of your love
I can remember
not letting go

# Sprinkling Desire

I relish in the sunshine
on your magical tongue

I savor the sentiments
on your flammable lips

I admire the sweetness
from your miraculous smile

I idolize the brightness
of your strength

I am fascinated by the glow
of your heartbeat

I cherish your fingertips
and your precious touch

I honor your intellect
and your neon kindness

I am attached to your
soothing voice

I appreciate your rainbows
and the edges of your heart

# Falling for a Sunrise

I'm falling
for a sunrise that
ignites a magical flame

I'm falling
for the brightness
of her scars

I'm falling
for her
enigmatic strength

I'm falling
for her truth
humanity and her genuine heart

I'm falling
for a sunrise that
shines so bright

I'm not afraid
of falling
I just fear
the height of the fall

# Falling into Twilight

Love her precious sky
Love her southern wind
Love her gentle soul
Love her divine tenderness
Fall into her light

Love her brilliant heart
Love her rare body
Love her stunning mind
Love her candlelit intuition
Fall into her wildflower

Love her innocent giggle
Love her inner child
Love her broken moon
Love her bashful sun
Fall into twilight

# Forever in the Afterglow

I want to suffocate in your bliss
I want to plunge into your beloved river
I want to soak up your sincerity
Open and let me find you

I fell for your afterglow
I want to be overwhelmed by your eyes
I want to sink in your palm
I want to be strangled by your affection
Open and let me see you

I fell for your silver tongue
I want to be enthralled by your charm
I want to consume your high flames
I want to sleep between your light and dark
Open and let me feel you

I fell for your enchanting universe
I want to soak up your character
I want to touch your insecurities
I want to kiss your lips of heaven
Open and let me listen to you

I fell for your wisdom dripping from you

# Weeping Daydreams

In your arms
I felt the shine of the sun

In your arms
I felt the overjoyed love

In your arms
I felt the emptiness fade

In your arms
I felt the perfect embrace

In your arms
I felt the daydreams weep love

In your arms
I felt our worlds be complete

In your arms
I felt us melt as one

In your arms
I felt your precious tears

In your arms
I felt our life begin

28

# Vows to an Angel

I stood between the dusk
and the shimmering light
I stared at the crescent of
the bellowing moons

As I sat there in a moment
of reflection
I could feel the teardrops of
an angel falls on my shoulder

She was more radiant
than a painting
She was more elegant
than a statue of gold

I fell in love with her
crying shadows
I fell in love with her
loneliness and cravings

As my hand touched
her cheekbone
I was overcome by joy
Fulfilled every threshold

of my beating and still heart
On bended knee
I wept in the river of love
Overflowing and cleansed

I reached for my quill
and the words poured out
like the rain from the bleeding sky
My undying love for a fallen angel

was cemented in my vows
Embraced in forever
Cherishing her like a poem
Placing the diamond on her

porcelain finger
Gentle like a China doll
Eternal flames surround our unity
Endlessly in love with a perfect soul

# Crooked Thunderbolts

Under a rainbow of shades of blue
I saw a glimpse of your golden smile
Staring at your freckles
I gaze into the storms of your eyes
Embracing crooked thunderbolts
I fell into your theatrical mist
Touching your sapphire core
I stumbled into a haze of echoing beauty
Repeating your name in my sleep
I adore your quiet skeletons
Admiring your drops of anguish
I hold you delicately in my arms
Falling madly in love with your spirit

# Basket of Gold

Hand in hand
Walking through the basket of gold
Surrounded by nature's scent
Barefoot and carefree
Like the precious love in our hearts
Hand in hand
Gripping tight refusing to let go
Appreciating the sound of her voice
Marveled by her addicting laughter
Whispering "PS I love you"
In her ear and kissing her neck
Under the hundred-year oak tree
Hand in hand
Realizing this hand is the only hand
I want to feel for a lifetime

# The Blush Vertebrae

Icicles of vulnerability
dangle over my crucified nerves
Leisurely indulging
a mass consumption of integrity
Thickening the backbone
Watching frustrations corrode
Tortuously eyeballing the poison
seep in my blush vertebrae
Struggling between the roar of
disarray and the calm light
Hacking up chunks of sincerity
Clearing my throat to voice
the sound of everlasting waves
from my vibrant spine
Drops of sorrow fall to my feet
Faith never misled my center

# Slowly

Slowly
I am beginning to resent you
Slowly
I can see that I was right
Slowly
I can recognize you don't have the strength
Slowly
I can see what you didn't hear
Slowly
I am seeing what I expected to happen
Slowly
I can see I hated being right
Slowly
I tried to give you the warnings
Slowly
I gave you everything you could want
Slowly
I am becoming ignored
Slowly
It shows you were not prepared

# STELLA WALKER'S ACQUAINTANCES

"Discover the distinction between friendships and acquaintances."

# Harper Mullins

I'm habitually shy and cautious
I'm serene and stuck in sentences
Excuse me, I'm in awe of you

I'm carefully hesitant and quiet
I'm placid and cemented in paragraphs
Excuse me, I admire you

I'm thoroughly fearful and discrete
I'm tentative and fastened in paraphrases
Excuse me, I adore you

I'm rationally reserved and hushed
I'm hesitant and jumbled in emotions
Excuse me, I cherish you

I'm gingerly modest and demure
I'm indecisive and scrambled in sentiments
Excuse me, I'm in love with you

# Sebastian Cage

Blade like teeth sparkle
Drooling a sinister circus
Vomiting chunks of truth
After inhaling gobs of deceit
Staring at shattered mirrors
stepping into shards of identity
Cutting into a split personality
A minor loss of hearing
Slick black Dracula like hair
Hanging his spirit like a bat
in a tortuous dying cave
As he plays a lullaby backwards
Hands quickly shrivel
Silent eyebrows howl
Character is a slow death

# Danielle Lee

Authentically jagged
Crisp maroon edges
Revved up by the throttle
Seductively mysterious
A provocative beast
Lover of Blackjack
Carrying lip biting hunger
Tattooed and strong
Mentally rough
Hardcore in all layers

# Matthew Trotter

Loves stacking blocks
Loves apples and pears
Loves Bugs Bunny
Loves hiding behind the chair
Loves to snuggle
Loves to turn pages
Loves to change his mind
Loves making messes
Loves his checkered blanket
Loves his stuffed monkey
Loves to make a hearty laugh
Loves to be a toddler
Loves his mother and father

# Debra Milton

She let out a crying whisper
She was terrified of the light
Waiting for him to answer

She ignored all the colors
She fell into the corner
Waiting for him to answer

She slept with the stranger
She hid from anyone close
Waiting for him to answer

She stared into alienation
She walked away from the signs
Waiting for him to answer

She ran from the shackles
She stood in the crossroads
Waiting for him to answer

She hobbled around midnight
She anticipated change of direction
Answers were always there

# Joshua Bratton

Defined by the dollar
Defined by possessions
Defined by quantity
Defined by numbers
Defined by the notches in the board
Defined by the color of the suit
Defined by the size of the house
Defined by brand names
Defined by his image
Defined by skewed perception

# Grace Beaumont

World class manipulator
A mind playing tramp
Money hungry and shallow
A body of pleasantries
Carrying a thousand pounds

of pulled and torn guilt
A first prize procrastinator
Fighting temptations
Alluring and magnetic
Horrifying addictions

Unable to love herself
Arrested for indecency
Shame stapled to her
worn out forehead
Pregnant and unstable

Mending all the pieces
Finally surrendering
to a higher almighty power
Watching an ocean of tears
Fall to the ground

Someone took her forgiveness
that she could no longer
bear and hold within
Releasing the thousand pounds
to take it day by day

# Stuart Bagley

Completely childish
A sophomoric sense of humor
Constantly wasting time
Goalless wanderer
A sack of potatoes on the couch
Wishing to live in a TV
Work not in vocabulary
Between his 20's and 30's
A bleak future
Relies too much on others
Lives in fantasy land
Scared of reality
Finally looking within

# Katrina Larkin

Additionally, I'm a babbling extrovert
Furthermore, I'm a cunning biologist
Above and beyond I'm cut-throat
I'm in conjunction with invisible integers

Display manners like an 18th century surgeon
Dissecting emotions like a psychologist
Sitting side by side with top notch analysts
Typically ignoring run on sentences

Extremely clinical in problem solving
Rational to digits, irrational behind doors
Walking with an exorbitant amount of energy
No consumption of lethal stamina drink needed

A well-known documented efficiency expert
Full of propositions and commotion
Slip inside my carnival enterprise like mind
Witchcraft in my sturdy right hand

A strong appetite for methodologies
Craving a cookie cutter and routine lover
Pareto charts in my tight left hand
Lack moxie and enthusiasm at moments

Intellectually driven by the power of knowledge
Scratch that, strive for the application
I'm the sun in the wintertime
Grin for the bewitching scientist

# Dana Blough

Born deceiver and storyteller
Creates havoc and consequences
Golden authentic fabricator
Generator of a wide web of deception
Original falsifier and con artist
A leader of noise and turmoil
Shaking cynical bloodhound
Dressed as a loud pretender
A misfit among the thieves
Wearing rebellion as a trench coat
A cold villain underneath

# Aralia Desmond

Fragile and quiet
Emotionally abused
Worthless painted
On all four walls
in tragic thick blood
Staring at the letters
Losing herself not
recognizing her
stunning beauty
Tormented and scarred
Rediscovering the
starlight qualities
in her mid-30's
Accepting her dim past
But rebuilt to be stronger
than ever before

# Erika Paxton

Slightly obsessed with perfection
Slightly troubled with cleanliness
Slightly infatuated with structure
Slightly engrossed with order
Slightly hooked with simplicity
Slightly hinged with framework
Slightly compelled with arrangements
Slightly fascinated with architecture
Slightly delighted with nature
Slightly charmed with documentaries
Slightly enchanted with socialism
Slightly enamored with practically
Slightly absorbed with philosophy
Slightly hypnotized with the bare minimum

# Ashton Kerr

Defies brick walls and flaming obstacles
Defies wailing authorities with bullets
Defies plastic and bold labels
Defies political rhetoric with a raised fist
Defies reckless wars without causes
Believes in thinking for yourself

Defies opinions being crammed down throats
Defies yellow charm with painted speeches
Defies religion but embraces holy spirits
Defies tattooed monkeys who nod their heads
Defies thoughts wrapped up in a cardboard box
Believes in thinking for yourself

Defies ignorance and emotional repetition
Defies hatred and destructive patterns
Defies being patronized and twisted sarcasm
Defies written fears and wooden nickels
Defies colored rejection with pointing fingers
Believes in thinking for yourself

# Rachel Madison

Soothing erotic voice
A tender but a hurricane of a soul
Roaming dark pastures
Absorbing nature
Delicate heartbeats
Alluring soft skin
Falling deep in her magical eyes
Playing within her diamond circus
Captivated by her perceptiveness
Appreciating her ocean tears
One exotic and magnificent woman

# Jackson Cash

A rugged southern charm
Potent as whiskey and honey
Personality dipped in marmalade
Attached is his magnetic intellect
A polarizing myth and superhero
Drowns in sensuality and appeal
Casting shadows of perfection
chiseled from head to toe
endearing and rich qualities
A man with a sense of wonder
laced in humility and honesty
Integrity tattooed to his rainbow soul
A warrior from the blazing sun
seeking humanity and kindness
waiting for his other half to melt his heart

# Bradford Stills

I'm bullheaded with spite between my teeth
Occasionally difficult and brittle
I play on the wrong side of danger
I should get a prize for being someone else

Stalking sounds of restlessness
Crude and subdued on the outside
Dabbling with strawberry temptations
I should get a prize for being someone else

Hollow and fragile on the inside
Frequently sleeping with exploitations
I'm regularly running from my demons
I should get a prize for being someone else

Blinking every two seconds frantically
Clutter and disarray seeping
I'm a wreck that no one wants to know
I should get a prize for being someone else

# Carmela Moss

A queen of sarcastic hearts
Withdrawn and cryptic
A gloomy black eye
from insomnia and anxiety
A condescending dancer
wearing stockings of
stretched-out distress
Fulfilling voids of for others
Defined by her name by
with twenty-dollar bills
Treating men as toys
with high expectations
Allowing her center
turn into granite

# Bryce Powers

The shaman of seduction
Ayatollah of luscious souls
The prince of pleasure
21st Century Don Juan
Physically focused
Creating an iconic body
Lean and trim
Muscle on muscle
Beautifully molded
60-minute man
The king of midnight

# Mia Amore

Enigmatic wandering light
A lost breath of fresh air
Profound and intellectual
A divine blacktop soul
Heart carved from clouds
A distant precious road
Fearless and troubled
A roaring laughter
Treasured candle of love
Dedicated and persistent
A wanderlust masterpiece
Blooming fascination
A secret admirer of her core

# Thompson Perry

Emphatically pretentious
Irrationally presumptuous
Consistently audacious
Logically constricted
Evidentially precarious
Clearly problematic
Constantly ambiguous
Borderline hazardous
Extremely indecisive
Ridiculously outlandish
Classically bizarre
Extraordinarily offbeat
Commonly erratic
Vividly unaccountable
Particularly mystifying
Undeniably perplexing
Typically, uncanny

# Jazz Brown

Gliding into a smog
Pouring firewater into a shot glass
Exchanging gossip over
mixed drinks wrapped around
a mesmerizing saxophone
Overheating remarks on Socrates

Reciting lines from the book of Proverbs
Observing the couple in the
Deep chocolate booth sipping
On luscious martinis and chain smoke
to the sound of the rhapsody
Entwined notes and soulful galore

Hypnotized to his shuffling feet
as he sways back and forth
nicknaming him Jazz Brown
An entertainer in the center of the heart
Playing for thousands over decades
Married to his sweet saxophone

# UNPAVED CROSSROADS

"Every road tells a story."

# Black and Blue on Devastation Road

She slid between the scattered distractions
If she had ran away from the distractions
If she dismissed the running lines on the wall
If she forgave herself for the vacancy

Black and Blue to the center
Smacked, punched, and beaten by a chameleon
"Today is the day, I walk away"
Self-worth is finally my fist

If she assumed the collision was delicate
If she harbored the watercolors in her heart
If she clenched on to the drops of unity
If she was quiet in the twilight

Black and Blue to the center
Smacked, punched, and beaten by a chameleon
"Today is the day, I walk away"
Self-worth is finally my fist

If she expressed the misery on the inside
If she climbed out of the madness
If she flickered like a light in the dark
If she surrendered to his commands

Black and Blue to the center
Smacked, punched, and beaten by a chameleon
"Today is the day, I walk away"
Self-worth is finally my fist

# Unforgettable Blue Eyes Lane

Never will I forget your palm
Never will I forget your kiss in the wind
Never will I forget your precious star
Never will I forget the crack in the pavement
Never will I forget the sparkling memories
Never will I forget your endless passion
Never will I forget the missing number from your mailbox
Never will I forget the calm sea in your eyes
Never will I forget the color of your door
Never will I forget the letter I read before you left
Never will I forget your wings of freedom
Never will I forget the faded sign

# Struggling on Carelessness Road

Destroyed trust smeared on shingles
Ruins spread out over the dismantled carpet
Locked up gates surrounding decrepit doors
Components of ancient clocks in disgust
Splinters in necks of apathetic voices
Arms folding like a hand of cards
Negligence lingers in the crisp air
Carelessness hobbling on a narrow path
Monotony standing tall and shrewd
Incuriosity bounces like a dodge-ball
Separation is coughed up like phlegm
Alienation is the divine appetite
Four-mile Road of still emptiness
Unfortunately, many reside in a glance of reality

# Fastened on Random Avenue

I took a sharp turn
down dishonesty lane
and witnessed corruption
I went around the bend
to discover a narrow
jealousy road

After the tunnel I drove
a hundred miles on
a wide-open faith road
I took a winding right
on the angry dirt path

I'm only fifty miles
away from Random Avenue
I was told I would see
Dancers, vigilantes, prostitutes,
and painters on the
brittle sidewalk

I would glance up at
shattered windows
and bronze slumbers
I will admit I was terrified
to travel down Random Avenue
and see the invisible scarecrows

Visualizing clenched hands to the
steering wheel feeling
the chaos and poverty
in the brisk air

# Wavering Wealth on Wall Street

Fluctuating economy
Stimulating Dow Jones
Buying and selling
In the eyes of the dollar sign

watching corporate America
Staring at bonds maturing
Building portfolios instead
of solid credibility

Complexity of convexity
Depreciating values
Staggering interest rates
Exploration of investments

Discussing volatile markets
Among a million decorated suits
Gripping risks and strapping
onto fixed incomes

Expecting returns on a rush
of thin adrenaline
Motivated by the number one root
of pure evil

# Wide Eyed on Cupid's Dream Drive

From the glistening waves
to the boundless shore
Strings of love dwell
in the enchanted violin

From the untamed daisies
to the serene marigolds
Appetites of wicked flames
burn in a pink stratosphere

From the beaming sunrise
to the caress of your hand
Admiration is a blazing star
above Cupid's Dream Drive

Shadows or darkness
become a lost road of lust
Only worship and devotion
entwine on this long concrete

# Stumbling on Overflowing Ink Boulevard

I saw vibrating rainbows
draped over a slippery moon.
I saw glitter on 20 x 20 frames.
I could hear the grand piano playing
in the deserted mountains

I saw a glimpse of red in the clouds of rage
I saw rivers of champagne.
I witnessed sorrow hiding
deep into the caves

I saw the sun bellow
I saw bouquets of silence seek Cupid's harp
fell into the well creeping
behind the parade of jesters

I saw the edges of souls
bleed tears of joy
I saw emptiness screech
I felt the warmth of diamond shaped hearts

I found a bottle of spilled ink
and the words were never ending
I heard trumpets around the bend
I saw blank pages but words
rattled and spoke like gospel

I discovered the path of humanity
I caressed the gentleness of others
I climbed into the vortex of raw emotions
I felt the infinite words in ink overflow within myself

# Falling on Cabrillo Avenue

I fell in love
with a broken soul
I fell in love
with her sunrise and sunset
I fell in love
with her wild animation

I fell in love
with her wick and poison
I fell in love
with her sharp blade
I fell in love
with her sensuous magic

I fell in love
with her burnt threshold
I fell in love
with her over the top style
I fell in love
with her distorted image

I fell in love
with her scrapes and bruises
I fell in love
with her brightness and mind
I fell in love
with her alluring voice

But her words destroyed me
and left me in emptiness
on Cabrillo Avenue

# Sweetness on Exhilaration Avenue

I've been in love with the nectar and the sour drippings of you
I've been captured by the glaze of your caress
I've been in awe by the comfort and the shivers of your embrace
I've been enamored by the never-ending kisses and the affection
I've been mesmerized by the sparkle dancing in your midnight eyes

And the love with you is breathtaking
And the love with you is indescribable
And the love with you is remarkable
And the love with you has opened me up

After so many years
I wouldn't have changed a second

I've been in love with the honey and the radiant treasures of you
I've been enchanted by your words and glamorous skin
I've been aching for the centerpiece to wake me up and feel alive
I've been daydreaming of an endless love
I've been intoxicated by the shimmering light twinkling in your soul

And the love with you is breathtaking
And the love with you is indescribable
And the love with you is remarkable
And the love with you has opened me up

After so many years
I wouldn't have changed a second

# Aspirations on Ten Chapters Lane

Here I am, I don't have followers
I have sanguine blisters and
indecisions stirring in my reckless mind
I've stood in the corridor of my considerations
and wide-eyed aspirations
I've been guided by intolerable vices,
 a stench of trivial knowledge and sarcasm
I have concoctions growing in my garden
I've borrowed money from my child like brother
to rent a house not far from the Porcupine River
We use to play like thieves, run like dogs,

and wrestle in the amber mud for hours
I live in a two-bedroom apartment,
One block away from the Midtown bakery
On Sunday's I can smell the Apple fritters
I've worked at the local grocery store since I was fifteen
"Lucky" isn't a word in my vocabulary
I bite my fingernails as I ponder in front of my 1971 typewriter
From 9pm to 10pm I'm a rapid reader
I fell in love with Mark Twain and
the storytellers from the innocent wild

Stuck on the lucid and elusive chapter ten
Captivated between the commas and engaging dialogue
I cough at the errors and sniffle at the page count
 of my thrill seeking novel
I stretch out my imagination like a rubber band
Manuscript growing like an oak tree
Here I am, born an offbeat writer
The people who know me stand distant
Afraid to crawl inside the brain of characters
I left my day job at the age of forty-two
Perspiration and diligence were on my side

# The Lost Goodbye on Adieu Street

I use to wear a serenading taxi cab colored sweatshirt
with a patch of birds heading south for the winter to Morgan's
house
She'd always laugh at the caption below
"Are we there yet?" and pour me a drink

She paraded her father's den that reeked of nicotine and late-
night affairs
Flipping through the eclectic taste of albums
Spinning the quarter in the afternoon air
Indecisiveness roaming like a soldier

Morgan was the advocate of passive aggressiveness
Mumbling curse words and playing with a rubber band in
tangled dialogues
Morgan would often lean in and tap her fingers
on my thigh as if she was playing the piano

Slightly obtrusive and deliberately coy
Consistently playing word games with my emotions
Shouting "Love is fickle, but you could dance with me for a
nickel"
Often devilish wearing a copper halo

Tossing idioms between stirred pauses
Blatantly ignoring the officer in the pictures on the olive walls
She referred to him as the man that dragged her from state to
state
Leaving her in decorated homes with meaningless jewelry

Constantly toying with closeness and distance with my lips in
the sanctuary
Shaking my head from the autumn perfume

From month to month my title changed from toolbox to
aberration
On that fateful hour I made the doorbell sing and no one replied

Glancing down at the welcome mat I picked up the ivory
envelope
Ramblings were engraved and cemented
Paragraphs leaving a starry-eyed melody
Entranced by the last line that catapulted reality

"The officer who claims to be my father hasn't taught me how to
say goodbye"

# And the Poet's Cry on Longfellow Road

I was born somewhere special but out of place
I was born with a slanted perception recognizing I don't fit in
I was born in a whirlwind of have-nots and could-have-beens
I was born with a cloud of imperfections that I can't see

And the metaphors stagger between the lines
And the allegories waddle between reality and delusions
And the observations hobble under the lemon sun
And the analogies stumble on the concrete
And the personifications shed vibrant skin

I was born too close to deserted fools playing for keeps
I was born feeling like an untouchable lover who's never felt
loved
I was born with a misguided star that refuses to shine
I was born with escapism in my pocket and fantasies in my hand

And the metaphors stagger between the lines
And the allegories waddle between reality and delusions
And the observations hobble under the lemon sun
And the analogies stumble on the concrete
And the personifications shed vibrant skin

I was born with freedom painted on walls but with frustrations
kept in a box
I was born italicizing my soliloquy and my anger written in
cursive
I was born to shout from four empty walls and silence
decorating my tongue
I was born with a eulogy written with a violent mist

And the metaphors stagger between the lines
And the allegories waddle between reality and delusions
And the observations hobble under the lemon sun
And the analogies stumble on the concrete
And the personifications shed vibrant skin

I was born to inhale iron sins dipped in ink to write my
biography
I was born to sleep with desires that my companion doesn't
want to hear
I was born to walk with obscurity on an empty path
I was born to dream vividly and live between black and white

And the metaphors stagger between the lines
And the allegories waddle between reality and delusions
And the observations hobble under the lemon sun
And the analogies stumble on the concrete
And the personifications shed vibrant skin

I was born with careless pupils with details left in the dusk
I was born in an atmosphere dancing with minutia
I was born with confrontation and commotion
I was born without a compass seeking direction endlessly

I was born with recklessness waving and stirring
I was born running from myself and toward complacency
I was born twisting paragraphs and contorting conversations
I was born a quiet extrovert seeking attention with mind
numbing fireworks

And the metaphors stagger between the lines
And the allegories waddle between reality and delusions
And the observations hobble under the lemon sun
And the analogies stumble on the concrete
And the personifications shed vibrant skin

# Tenderness on Effervescent Lane

Sweet Ophelia,
Out of morbid curiosity
Are your lingering shadows in disbelief
Bitter tongue bound and burned
The scent of your scars never learned

Sweet Ophelia,
Between your warmth and generosity
How can you be in love with me
Sadness is a hummingbird in my eyes
Broken down with armor in disguise

"She deserves more than I could ever give,
But she clenches on to me as long as we both shall live,
Neither of us know what we deserve,
With her by my side, I can see my worth"

Sweet Ophelia,
Inside this snowflake feel the monstrosity
Are you afraid I will be the one to leave
Fear is the calm wrapped around my bones
Whispering "you are my center and my home"

Sweet Ophelia,
Of all the treasures and the uncertainty
Faith is trusting in the power of what you can't see
How can you love a man who doesn't love himself
For I have forgiven the stars, nothing else

"She deserves more than I could ever give,
But she clenches on to me as long as we both shall live,
Neither of us know what we deserve,
With her by my side, I can see my worth"

# Sentiments of Baker Street

Distraught and clutching on to pieces
Staring into the incoherent past
Wandering down Baker Street with heaviness
Overlooking the restless water at Vera Creek
Caught between the isolation and jitters

Wounds reopen after a silent decade
Discussions flickering inside the storm
Between the rapid sting and the convulsions
Sorrow stretches across my empty face
Turning the knob of the Morning Bird Cafe
Recognizing the clock on his face
Standing up to see arms spread wide

An overwhelming hug fills the air
Bond between a flower-like daughter
and a run-down tin can of a father
Apologies and regrets tossed into the burning azure
Capturing the sentiments and affection

# Painting Wildflower Lane

Under her breath she uttered "Life is as beautiful as a forehead
kiss"
Joy dances like a ballerina on her spellbinding tongue
She squeezed tea parties with her doll Delilah with her artistry

Quietly adoring her childhood books on the shelf from the tallest
to the shortest
She painted love with the ocean with her steady hand on her
prized canvas

Gazing at her innocent imagination
Memorized the pattern and pastel colors of her quilt
In a whisper she mumbled "Beauty is inside, not in the eye of the
beholder"

Climbing inside her mellow perception
She glided across the beige carpet with an ornament of a smile
A sphere filled with crayons, lite-bright, easy bake oven, and
ballroom dresses

Cherishing the extraordinary recollection,
Embracing the collage of photographs in her heart
Drops fall to the floor as she glances at a hollow room on
Wildflower Lane

# Standing on Love's Dreamscape Lane

I thought love was a bouquet of never-ending dreams
I thought love was a ghost that never left me
I thought love was a sky that I could stare at all day
I thought love was a splash of memories painted on a canvas
I thought love was a stain between the sheets

I thought love was a mist and a waterfall at the same time
I thought love was a butterfly chasing the morning rainbow
I thought love was a photograph of kisses
I thought love was conversations until sunset
I thought love was a nervous condition

I thought love was a blue jay flying in the sky
I thought love was a bowl of cherries
I thought love was a drug no one could ever purchase
I thought love was the overused pen
I thought love was the center of the universe

I thought love was the underused verb
I thought love was the rain on the window
I thought love was a hug and a forehead kiss
I thought love was the scent on your pillow
I thought love was when we held hands on our first walk

I thought love was when you were on my mind all day
I thought love was when you randomly said "I love you"
I thought love was when I was a want and not a need
I thought love was a fear of feeling
I thought love was a light in the dark

I thought love was the scarf worn in the cold
I thought love was more than hand gestures
I thought love was unforgettable and forever

I thought love was something I would feel
I thought love was more than just wearing a wedding ring

I thought love was immeasurable and pain was measurable
I thought love was a note stuck on the vanity
I thought love was filling and would never know empty
I thought love was something I wouldn't feel
I thought love was a fantasy I had as a child

I thought love was a spectacle and a miracle
I thought love was a recipe of tenderness and trust
I thought love was everything until someone made it nothing
I thought love was a dream that would never end
I thought love was priceless until someone threw it away

# Love's Nightmare Lane
## (Parallel to Love's Dreamscape Lane)

Love was just an insignificant occupant making me gag
Love was just a bad joke I heard in another language I couldn't
comprehend
Love was just a citizen that held me down and raped my soul
with a jagged knife
Love was just a stench I couldn't wash out
Love was just a word created by Hallmark

Love was just four letters thrown together to serve a ridiculous
purpose
Love was just a shadow so I can feel myself
Love was just a bruise on my shin to prove I exist
Love was just a song written by a billion-dollar jester
Love was just a death wish waiting in the wings

Love was just a plant I didn't water
Love was just a black eye with covered up lies
Love was just a watercolor I can't see
Love was just mascara running down my face
Love was just a cloud of obscurity

Love was just a gram and a kilo of voids
Love was just a room of emptiness
Love was just a shattered mirror I look at every day
Love was just a pile of poems that made sense one day
Love was a just a pile of poems that I threw away the next

Love was just an adolescent that claimed to know it all
Love was just an adult with an addiction that didn't know a
damn thing
Love was just a bomb that exploded on planes, in buildings, and
in schools

Love was just a clan, cult, gang, a war of losses
Love was just a book that millions don't read

Love was just a doctrine of stolen beliefs
Love was just a pile of divorce papers
Love was just a trigger pulled by one finger as the other four
were staring at him
Love was just an overused word
Love was just ten minutes of casual sex

Love was just an irrational scream
Love was just the sun not seeing the moon
Love was just a tragedy in a brilliant disguise
Love was just a down payment for an item I haven't touched
Love was just a puzzle piece that doesn't seem to fit anywhere

# Alone on Jacks River Road

I witnessed a revolution within my evolution
Blending between the escape and noise
Seeking a discrete language within my bones
Torn into shrapnel and self-diluting conflict

"Son, you can never walk away from the pain
Don't bother trying if your mindset is the same
We all have to fall to see where we are
It takes a lifetime to recognize what was easy and what was
hard"

Thirty-five years passing by,
Staring at the same rooms with the same old eyes
Points of view turned me into stone
It's not a secret that I'm walking alone

I've held a reputation to ignore the sensation
A fusion of mediocrity and ignorance
Hunting down a passage in a coma
Frayed and twisted in my frozen mind

"Son, you can never change what was
Don't bother trying to walk off the buzz
We all have to crawl before we can run
It takes a lifetime to recognize what you've become"

Thirty-five years passing by,
Staring at the same rooms with the same old eyes
Points of view turned me into stone
It's not a secret that I'm walking alone

# The Handwriting on Innocence Crossing

I grew up on dirty folklore and clean superstition
I grew up living with a Kentucky gambler and shadows sleeping
in my bed
I grew up next to the iridescent wind and southern chimes
ringing in my ears
I grew up listening to Charlie Daniels and the violin in my soul


And she cries "Turn the radio up and drown in self-love"


I danced in my imagination
Wrapped up in all of sensations
Between the words and in the lines
Fell in love with the books and the peace in my mind
And the inspiration thickened...


I grew up on self-preservation with the moonlight glaring
through my window
I grew up on the sounds of logic playing in the background
I grew up on the fears tucked away and pride stained on my chest
I grew up rinsing the doubt and washing away the madness


And she cries "Turn the radio up and drown in self-love"


I danced in my imagination
Wrapped up in all of sensations
Between the words and in the lines
Fell in love with the books and the peace in my mind
And the inspiration thickened...


I grew up on faith worn like a torn glove
I grew up on hope stuffed in my pockets of my ripped jeans
I grew up on obscurity sitting on the rocking chair of my porch
I grew up on affection displayed two times a year

And she cries "Turn the radio up and drown in self-love"

I danced in my imagination
Wrapped up in all of sensations
Between the words and in the lines
Fell in love with the books and the peace in my mind
And the inspiration thickened.

# Disoriented on Dead End Avenue

I can't explain the azaleas growing in my fading garden
I can't explain the degrading writing on my flaming wall
I can't explain the lack of intuition on the inside
I can't explain the tossing and turning in my decaying bed

Daphne Bridges, I can't find my wallet and don't know where I am
Daphne Bridges, I can't find my home and
don't know where I'm going

I can't explain the bronze on my tired arms sitting in the shade
I can't explain the sorrow drifting like a cloud above me
I can't explain the bullets sitting in my dresser drawer
I can't explain the screams I locked in a jar
I can't explain the joker and ghost laughing in my closet

Daphne Bridges, I can't find my wallet and don't know where I am
Daphne Bridges, I can't find my home and
don't know where I'm going

I can't explain the ringing in my eardrum
I can't explain the fear running down my spine
I can't explain the sickness in my stomach
I can't explain the emptiness in my hand
I can't explain the phantom dancing in my head

Daphne Bridges, I can't find my wallet and don't know where I am
Daphne Bridges, I can't find my home and
don't know where I'm going

# In Slow Motion on Universe Road

That's the way the addiction grumbles
That's the way the drunk stumbles
That's the way the moon serenades
That's the way the elephants walk in the parade
That's the way the politicians talk
That's the way the predators gawk

That's the way the innocent dream
That's the way the raped scream
That's the way the fears surrender
That's the way the cold remembers
That's the way the lost are found
That's the way the veterans weep to the sounds

That's the way the truth should be told
That's the way the lies are bitten and sold
That's the way the victim cries
That's the way the quiet feel inside
That's the way the impregnator stares
That's the way the son of a bitch cares

That's the way the glass is poured
That's the way the children are ignored
That's the way the perception is skewed
That's the way the label is crude
That's the way the society thinks
That's the way the one percent drink

That's the way the air becomes stale
That's the way the skin becomes pale
That's the way the poets write
That's the way the day turns into night
That's the way the heart breaks into bits
That's the way the last puzzle piece fits

That's the way the thunder growls
That's the way the thieves prowl
That's the way the light disappears
That's the way the dark becomes crystal clear
That's the way the luck falls
That's the way the anger crawls

That's the way the perpetrators finger points
That's the way the hippies smoke a joint
That's the way the teacher dresses
That's the way the students make messes
That's the way the winners gloat
That's the way the captain steers the boats

That's the way the rich treat the poor
That's the way the small companies close its doors
That's the way the snake rattles
That's the way the beast fights in battle
That's the way the cookie crumbles
That's the way the insider fumbles

That's the way the performers act
That's the way the sky becomes black
That's the way the song is heard
That's the way the villains see the words
That's the way the view turns into stone
That's the way the virtuous become alone

That's the way the branch breaks

# GROWL FROM THE SUN

"No stone is left unturned.
There are no sides and no labels."

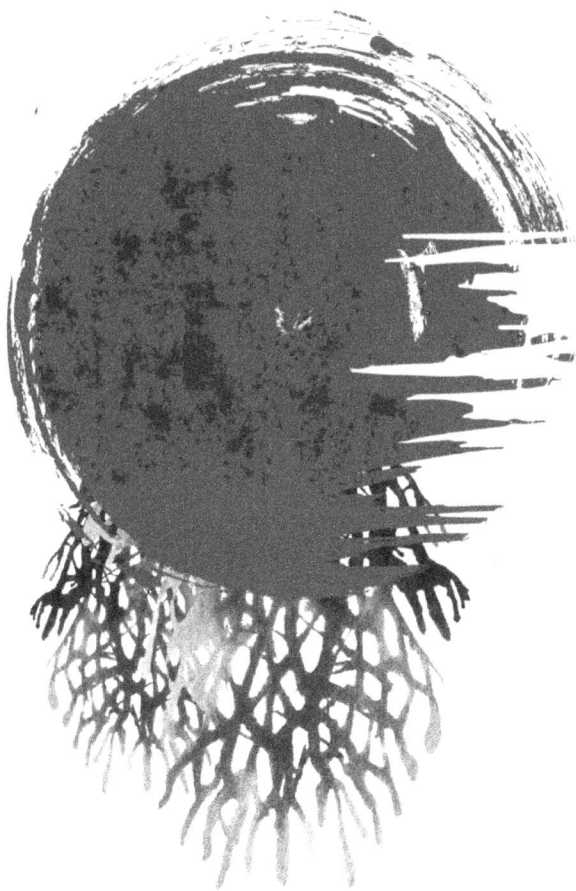

# No Subscription Necessary

I don't subscribe to your pathological illness dressed in authority
I don't subscribe to your ideologies wrapped up in restrictions
I don't subscribe to your strategies with ten-inch holes
I don't subscribe to your dogma with a stench

And in fine print "the manufacturer is not liable
or responsible"

The fraudulent news is at your fingertips
but the death count of mass consumption isn't

I don't subscribe to your cruel and savage intentions
I don't subscribe to your ferocious and flawed design
I don't subscribe to your diabolical scheme dipped in cyanide
I don't subscribe to your divide and conquer methodology

And in fine print "the manufacturer is not liable
or responsible"

The fraudulent news is at your fingertips
but the death count of mass consumption isn't

# Growl from the Sun

I

I'm glaring at an absent generation
minds glued to screens, tabloids,
Improving technology to do less
exercising depreciating value
at a ridiculous and outrageous rate
waving at the growl of the sunrise
four to six times a year, if that
operating like a business losing funds

I'm gawking at the disappearing
fundamentals, the backbone of humanity
digress, blaming the collapse of
civilization, pointing fingers at plastic
leadership, ignorance tattooed from
head to toe, wearing air pods to only
hear the agendas cloaked in madness
environmentalists shaking their heads
"listening" was just a nomadic word
fumbling around like a homeless man
sipping on vodka from his rustic flask

And the billions can feel the blisters
on their lackadaisical and passive feet
from the furious sun that hides behind
sinister clouds, rattle me off that diabolical
speech with spite beaming in your eyes
I can see our enemies' juggling bullets
and nuclear warfare with a legislative grin
where the truth is hidden, lies are contagious
speaking from both sides of the mouth
camouflaging motives and authenticity

I have witnessed the formation of the
surface world order, removing shovels,
eyebrows not raised, accepting mediocrity
I am surrounded by mosquitoes, snakebites,
takers, and a symphony playing in the
background of reality where the screams
are silent and the violence is obscene

I walk throughout the forest to seek peace
but only to discover the fall of humanity
"Borrow, borrow, borrow, we will pay the
high interest tomorrow, and forevermore"
the economy fluctuates, bargains with salespeople,
 trades with allies, shakes hands
with the murderers, and the sun boils like it's
sitting on a hot stove at 6:30pm in suburbia
waiting for a mother of three to throw in
a pound of rigatonis to cook,
run down and tired from the six hours
of restless sleep working
two jobs, patiently hanging for her ex-husband
to knock on her sanguine door
to hand her as a child support check
that will most likely bounce
And the children develop atrocious habits,
slightly dysfunctional, erratic behavior,
 struggling in school, and the therapy bill
shows up three months past due
And she can't pay that, saving nickels
 and dimes to take her joker like ex back to court

And the cycle of justice, lack of law
spins like a carousel without any pauses
education slowly slipping out the pyramid
degrees acquired through sixty-five-inch tvs

while paperback books became archaic
illiteracy, comprehension, critical thinking,
tossed into a body bag and thrown into
the bloodhound River by hundred thousand
dollar jesters playing as puppet masters
dictating, removing "history", deciding
on relevance, worth and silver dollar merit

Suits and paisley ties, accountants, who fixate
on numbers lack the ability to "understand"
people, individuals, and civilians

And the sun cringes at the decision makers,
narcissists behind a desk, keep drinking the
Devil's urine, believe in your hypocrisy
your bed is on the bottom floor breathing
in his arrogance and his cryptic verbiage

I've glanced at the complexity of relationships
but see the shade of nuances in simplicity
break down the triangle into savoring sections
remove the minutia, erase the routine
create mouthwatering memories, frame the
watercolors of the kisses and fragments of
the beloved tears, surrender to the emotions
light up humanity with an endearing greeting
extract the labels of humans, classify and only
subjects, things, and objects not individuals
advertise nothing, be who you are, be the magnet,
collect the pieces that make you whole,
ignore the punch lines, block out the
negativity, embrace the smiles,
make new beginnings and say goodbye to the nerve
crashing endings, celebrate life, the seconds,
move forward, don't sit still, rely on your instincts,

love your shadow, and never stop dreaming
be who you want to be, grow from the sunshine

I steer clear from the plexiglass propaganda,
narrow minded narrative and the acidic agenda
I chuckle and smirk at the raised clenched fist

In my peripheral vision, I can see the dancing tricksters,
articulate magicians, and the monotone zombies
pacing on the streets, I am a stained bystander,
observing the division, but put the universe under a
microscope and visually see God's hand
holding the earth with tears falling from his
cheek, I can hear him whisper a few words,
but the only clear word I grasp is "rapture"

I can see tragedies thrown into junkyards
due to corporations believing anything
and everyone is expendable and has a price
And the sun turns its head, no longer in front
of the vast kingdom we speak about
And the sun disappears like an unspoken ghost
hibernating from the turbulent storms

I scoffed at the down dressed pan handler
that quietly entered his Mercedes Benz between
Delusive Avenue and Excrement Road
I wasn't startled to hear the egos of
pin stripped suits brag about what they owned

I drive by the boarded-up apartments that
have been empty for a decade but
filled with rats and carry a stench for endless miles
I scan the faded newspaper of the property owner
who lives in a palace who is liable for the boxed up?
belittled residence, slightly haunted and eerie

I recognize empty fields, hollow playgrounds,
clear parks, and trees that don't hear a word
leaves blowing away, hushed, and dampened,
melancholy drips into the creeks, fear deepen
ideologies hit a threshold, spirituality is a fog
serenity is crawling, chaos and havoc strut
hand in hand, cynicism is filling the air,
humanity generating the poisonous pollution

II

I can foreshadow a society crumbling
from applied science, twisting theories
contorted plasma and friction analysis
thesis based on wealth and leaking myths
Pillars from a system situated in sand
a sinking infrastructure, vanishing unity
colorless pupils plagued with a manuscript
spineless leaders, particles of blunders piling up,
giant omissions paralyzing the fabric,
Programmed illnesses with a pinch of
annihilation, nations weeping counterfeit
drops of sadness, gradually seeking
contemporary alliances, executive orders
bleeding extermination, outlined syndromes
with a hint of illusions, corruption in the palms
 of the establishment, enigmatic statistics
catapulted in an ocean of the deceased

And the nerves of the vicious are numb
mankind's existence dwells in an experiment
And I can't feel the rays of the crying sun

I saw a glimpse of paradise, toddlers playing with
brilliance, wonder, and a light breeze serenading

through the air as a teenager
drinking water from fire hydrants, in front
of provincial chateaus, clarity, and modesty
was a thread, surrounded by a crooning sky
of beliefs and faith, conviction is just an
antique sitting in a clammy basement,
wrapped up in newspaper with headlines
of World War Two, buried in a crate labeled
"Precious and few", where dreams shifted, echoed
and the revolution within was smoldering,
 freedom was sung by entrepreneurs, capitalists,
and poetry was
a blue jay flying from tree to tree, love was
a drink we all consumed and sipped all through
the decorated nights, yet today the clowns
wear painted tears and smiles are weary

And the nerves of the vicious are numb
mankind's existence dwells in an experiment
And I can't feel the rays of the crying sun

I am madly in love with the metaphors from
Walt Whitman, sweetness waltzing through Dickinson's verses,
where landscapes feel the sunlight,
rain drizzling on white picket fences,
I fell for the similes that left glitter on my fingertips,
ballads that reverberate within the words,
stanzas that capture charm,
but in the present, I read a direct message,
thoughts thrown on paper within seconds,
impressions not thought provoking,
 automation becomes a crutch,
loneliness seeking attention, reality drifting like a hitchhiker,
dwindling patience, crime rising like flames in death-wish fields,
scarecrows parading cracked pavement,

insanity yells, neon lights flicker every three minutes,
like an apocalypse, but keep your view on the illuminating
screen,
sarcasm spasms, bellies filled with microwaved meals

And the nerves of the vicious are numb
mankind's existence dwells in an experiment
And I can't feel the rays of the crying sun

I've seen grownups stomp their feet,
throw childlike tantrums over slim debates
with cursed words thrown like daggers
I've seen electronic devices used to record
heinous crimes, satirical protests, and
mind bending disturbances across the globe
videographers portraying innocence,
displaying evidence, defending irresponsibility
I've seen switchblades pulled out over
loose change and collected indifferences
I've seen incompetency to be irrelevant,
tenure a driving force, dynasties collapsing
I've seen bewilderment shine brighter
than quickness and keen observations
I've seen enlightenment and murky insight
wither in closets at a candlelit masquerade

And the nerves of the vicious are numb
mankind's existence dwells in an experiment
And I can't feel the rays of the crying sun

III

I'm scrawling, swept away from the discord,
pleading to the amber crescent, hanging in the
audacious sky, gazing at the mindless clones,
no dismay of what will become, aggravation

turns into stone, eyelashes curve into dust,
puddles of demise, a graphite cyclone revolving around the fall,
a population relinquishing to the avalanche, I scowl to the
prognosis,
hindsight is rubble, my conjecture is not a conspiracy,
veracity is underneath the facade, I refuse to swallow the debris,
I trash the publications, I displace the buzzards,
I ignore the indoctrination, I carry my drum,
I am the feather that flies with placid eyes,
I don't place stamps on foreheads

To the awaken moon, I give you a letter of a thousand reasons
To the awaken moon, I am fond of your glow
To the awaken moon, I send you a letter to pass on to the
unconscious sun

To the helpless sun, the indifference is a path to nevermore,
but show us your sparkle, we pine for your radiance, numbness
is not your color,
your rays are in mourning, the lechery is within the choice,
the preference to wear blinders, floundering into traps,
shuffling excuses, pardon the shallow, explanation with holes,
to the sun you are not accountable

I'm scrawling, furiously with an ambiguous message,
forgive the gratuitous cyborgs, deception and the distortion
were carved,
the falsehood was chiseled, sculpted by self-centered dastards,
mercenaries injecting conflict with psychological warfare,
no intersections, a blueprint of disjuncture,
a frazzled atmosphere, frayed and stripped,
scoundrels running ramped, policies dipped
into indulgence, documents soaked in disarray,
I lean into the incoherent ramblings, methodical
studies forged, verbatim tampered with spots of evasion,

defamation spreading like a sickness, I refuse to consume the
Prozac,
paragraphs bellow with an enriched voice

To the awaken moon, I give you a letter of a thousand reasons
To the awaken moon, I am fond of your glow
To the awaken moon, I send you a letter to pass on to the
unconscious sun

To the forlorn and damaged sun, please shimmer where there is
darkness,
let the gleam fill in the crevices, please shimmer where pieces are
lost,
let the air rejoice in your magic, please be the aspiration to the
cosmos,
you are the enlightened preservation, you are the marvelous
treasure,
without you there is no growth, to the sun you are not accused
for the increased vibrations of the earth

IV

And I tumbled for the architecture of the
cathedrals across the United States,
And the bricklayers who cemented spirituality
but shouted from rooftops at the turtle
pace of change among all the religions
And I found the backbone of faith and hope
relies on the individuals silver wisdom
"Experience" breaks or defines conviction
And loyalty just doesn't reside in a chapel
I pray for the dying in my queen size bed
blending creed and politics is a toxic brew
And I cherished the artistic expressions on
the tarp, I was once fond of the textures
of our melting pot, I could taste the spices

and the tranquility, I use to take walks
in the garden of glee and feel the gust

But now the commander in chief raises
his disturbing hands, disrespecting our
ancestors, crippling the population,
And the sun bursts through the smog
with fury, the outbreak surges in the wind

The note is rejected…
"Embrace all the materialism, self-righteous possessions,
gold and glitter, let the poison
eat your soul, feel the edges of your heart
burn, you prioritized your choices, the angels left you a long
time ago"

I can't weep for the wicked and vicious
I can't weep for the manipulating tycoon
I can't weep for the shallow ministry
I can't weep for the blatant facade
I can't weep for the glowing charades
I can't weep for the brazen frontage
I can't weep for the vibrant myths
I can't weep for the singing deception

And the chill in the air reeks of self-indulgence
insects crawling on infectious patriarchs
but numb from the riddles of greed
spewing a language of hatred and fear
And tearing into the poverty-stricken class
gazing out into the seas of madness
And the wrecking machine, mechanisms, and
the machinery used to oversee the mass
It's the weapon and invisible bomb slithering
inside every human nervous system

You cry out safety and protection, misleading
from your glass throne, step by step you are entering your
exodus,
your skin is exiled but your veins are hollow,
calling yourself a leader, rushing to dismantle and depopulate
And the piece of the massacre lies within you

But now the commander-in-chief raises
his disturbing hands, disrespecting our
ancestors, crippling the population,
And the sun bursts through the smog
with fury, the outbreak surges in the wind

The note is rejected…
"Embrace all the materialism, self-righteous possessions,
 gold and glitter, let the poison
eat your soul, feel the edges of your heart
burn, you prioritized your choices, the angels left you a long
time ago"

I can weep for the innocent
I can weep for the fighters and warriors
I can weep for the fearless soldiers
I can weep for the sobbing children
I can weep for the unheard prayers
I can weep for the melody I never heard
I can weep for the deserving souls
I can weep for the fathers and mothers

And the sun will forever moan behind the clouds
And technology will continue to evolve
And God will remain quiet until the day he returns

# Left-Handed Twitch

I sat in the calm meadows, crossed my legs
contemplating the yin and the yang of society
differences are slippery, inequality widens
labels segregate, division tasting like salt

An unnecessary spice, over consumed
I could only see fragments, bits of humanity
traces of destruction in supermarkets,
shelves of products with the stamp "eat this"

prisons full of freedom fighters, locked up
for conviction, education systems funded by
non degree salespeople of social media,
economics is just a dart thrown at a polluted

sky, and I could feel the drops of sarcasm
landing on my notebook, where the poetry of
political tapestry was woven in city hall
Claims of unison is fraudulent, Build back Better

was just a slogan from the Left Hand
twitching and slapping the public across the face,
advertising peace but a bully at heart

# Criminal Logic
## (Fraudulent and Deadly Administration)

If you aren't liable, myths are woven in your institution
If you aren't liable, humans are quietly sacrificed
If you aren't liable, your establishment must have cobwebs
 in your dungeon
If you aren't liable, you must be contaminated
and crooked

Approved but not Accountable, criminal logic

If you aren't liable, you must have something to seek and
destroy
If you aren't liable, the outcome will be silenced
and remain a secret
If you aren't liable, your soul must have a hidden price tag
If you aren't liable, the war against the machine will continue

Approved but not accountable, criminal logic

If you aren't liable, the carcasses will disappear
into the darkest oceans
If you aren't liable, a slip up, a mistake is
crawling like a python
If you aren't liable, a vindictive counselor is on your side
If you aren't liable, the mystery must be a mirage
in your skewed vision

Approved but not accountable, criminal logic

# Ode to Freedom

Pardon me -
Wouldn't you like to hear a wistful melody?
a song with a cry from the underprivileged
strumming my amber acoustic guitar
I stand on the corner plucking with
melancholy dripping from my soul
repeating the heartbroken chorus

"Not one, not two, not three
But millions can see your lies
The people who support you
are paid for, are already dead inside"

And I'm playing for my children
And I'm playing for countless soldiers
And I'm playing for the light of freedom

Pardon me -
Wouldn't you like to hear a somber ballad?
lyrics that bleed sorrow and disunion
strumming with a speechless face
I stand on the corner singing with fragments
A solemn air floating in a tragic wind
repeating the grief-stricken chorus

"Not one, not two, not three
But millions can see your lies
The people who support you
are paid for, are already dead inside"

And I'm playing for my grandchildren
And I'm playing for my brothers in a war
And I'm playing for the candle of freedom

# Television is an Empty Prostitute

Television is a disturbance of luster and plentiful
Television is a scandalous invention
Television is a disruptive mechanism clogging
your arteries
Television is a vacuum sucking the cells
 from your cerebellum

And the imagination crumbled
And the ingenuity succumbs
And she seduces hour by hour

Television is nerve gas crippling your
 legs and motivation
Television is an apparatus blended with
hype and inferior hogwash
Television is a machine gun of information
 with a steering wheel
Television is a junkyard of contraband
 with sounds of justification

And the mind evaporates
And the muscles sit
And she seduces hour by hour

Television is a volatile substance with a grin
Television is a crutch with a bomb chained to your feet
Television is fifty-two-inch rectangle civilians idolize
Television is a glass religion with no faith

And she seduces hour by hour

# I'm Overpaid to Say Nothing

I decline to comment on cluttered cyberspace
I decline to comment on the illegal millions
flooded into our country
I decline to comment on the man made
infection generated in a lab

I decline to comment on the bigotry spreading
from our Neanderthal authorities in charge
I decline to comment on the enormous executive orders issued
I decline to comment on the irrational incompetence
and mind-boggling decisions

I decline to comment on my salary
and the zero percent of contribution to society
I decline to comment on those who raise
our national debt but don't pay taxes
I decline to comment on the election

that was stolen from the traditionalists
I decline to comment on our broken-down infrastructure
that our establishment ignores
I decline to comment on the proportion of lies
are greater than the absolute truth

I decline to comment on why our administration
blames everyone but themselves
I decline to comment on how the needle is just a tool
to reshape the economy across the universe
I decline to comment on those who shred your

beliefs because of their insecurities
I decline to comment on those who
were called monsters and fear mongers
I decline to comment, well I didn't I have nothing else to read
Like my superior, I can't think for myself

# Lost Referendums

I will cast my ballot
where nightmares boil, culture wars are
staged, dogs are experiments, politicians
are scientists, information is removed,
fact checkers endorse glaring falsehoods

I will cast my ballot
where parents are terrorists, freedom is a
coat, ignorance is idolized, tolerance is a
quilt, money laundering is kosher, fear is
instilled, and your opinion is irrelevant

where civilians are broken and referendums
are lost

I will cast my ballot
where certainty is muzzled, contradictions are cradled,
deficit skyrockets, gangs of immigrant's stampede,
inflation balloons, capitalism on life support, morals diminish

I will cast my ballot
where ignorance is air, negotiations are black,
wishes would vanish, labor shortages hike, social engineering is
secluded,
radicalism is ridiculous, and prosperity carries a gun

where civilians are pieces and votes are disregarded

I will cast my ballot
where prejudices are sipped, irresponsibility's
are embraced, wallets are empty, loans are neglected,
choices are out of reach, vultures are on billboards, bigots are
glorified

I will cast my ballot
where carpetbaggers sit on the curb, checks
and balances no longer exist, clear and present
danger is limping, speeches are spoken from
both corners of their mouth, ideologies spit

where civilians aren't the focal point and authorities have
shattered the system

# Party of Hate

Inside the catastrophic zoo
the centrist alters deception and veracity
the devious clan screams ugly slurs
stepping on each vulgar bureaucrat
partisans swallowing spoiled backlash
fingers declaring, infrastructure wobbling
lawmakers paralyzing the disjuncture
chatty pencil pushers, dollar sign hungry
A stench within the party of hate

# Tax Ramblings

Between the filing status and capital gains
words from the rich trample the poor
Among the billion deductions yanked
from stolen pockets splatter
Comparing gross income from the net is an eye opener
Taxes designed to be temporary stand like
skyscrapers in the 21st century

Pennies, nickels, and dimes depreciate
Cost of living increases are at sea level
Charitable contributions and tax credits spill like ink
Exemptions chuckle with a glass of champagne
Middle class filing receives a happy meal
Lack of filing forces Americans to acquire an orange wardrobe
Allowances and adjustments are worn like dresses

Annuity piling up like autumn leaves in the backyard
Dropping my case of beer is checked marked as a casualty loss
Dividends smiling and applauding like a crowd
FICA, an acronym to pay retired congressperson yearly salaries
Fringe benefits disappearing and wandering
Indirect and direct tax boxing in the ring
Dreading and head swaying to spring season

# FOR YOU, LOVE ALWAYS

"Drown in the reverberation of desire and every shade of love."

# The Sunflower's Breeze

I fell between the pages of an old love story,
where the fears drip from a morning hymn
clouds are reckless and clichés are terrified
I found myself captivated by the nuances,
echoes of solace bellow and the dreams
in her hand disperse out into the nightfall

You are the comfort in the dark
You are the vine I reach for
You are the sunflower's breeze in my eyes

I became infatuated with her innocence,
caught in a web of mixed catastrophes
where the fixations turned into addictions
and the atmosphere drizzles joy and drops
of gratification, I surrendered to her penumbra,
I slipped into a haze of affection and lust

You are the sunset in my daydream
You are the enchanted sea of grace
You are the sunflower's breeze in my eyes

A delicate sound of a violin, where tragedies are treasured and
the sounds of the wind seek out the mysteries of the beloved rain
I woke up in verses where desire was a thousand candles,
I venture into the slipstream and wait until the dragonflies
prowl for her shivering spirit

You are the exhilaration in my puzzle
You are the jewel in my obscure soul
You are the sunflower's breeze in my eyes

I find myself between the insatiable chapters
and the anxiety that twitches in the shade of the ancient tree,
I continue to ink and pour out the heartache I once ignored
forgive me twilight, I am fond of your crippled and fractured stars
I will follow your smeared moon

You are the magic in my stratosphere
You are the sugar fascination in my carousel
You are the sunflower's breeze in my eyes

I whisper softly into your white knuckled storms,
I want to be your thunder and crave for you to be my lightning,
I gasp on the devotion and tenderness,
I grasp for your fragile and soothing reverberation,
I long for your rapture and invincible glow,
I will chase your gloom

# Beautifully Broken

She walked into the rhythm
of the unspoken dance
She walked into a breeze
that illuminated her glow

She left California to feel another sun
She walked into a haze that
became clear from her scars
She walked into the word loyalty

and never looked back
She left happiness without a choice
She walked into the phrase "come here"
with a luscious smile

She walked into the candles of hope
to give her a glimpse of her future
She left summer to stand in a chill
She walked into the morning rain
without an umbrella to embrace the sensitivity

She walked into a pale sky seeking colors
that would make her stronger
She left a chapter struggling to turn the pages
still looking beautiful

# Forevermore Entwined

Repeatedly, she is exceptionally pleasant
periodically, she is dashing and divine
consistently, she is punctual and independent
constantly, she is kind-hearted and gentle
frequently, she is considerate and tender

Forevermore, my heart is entwined with hers

typically, she is good natured and authentic
regularly, she is merciful and generous
habitually, she is sympathetic and gracious
customarily, she is courteous and courageous
naturally, she is appealing and engaging

Forevermore, my heart is entwined with hers

normally, she is forgiving and affectionate
routinely, she is loyal and reverent
usually, she is remarkable and caring
ordinarily, she is thoughtful and devoted
commonly, she is delightful and amiable

Forevermore, my heart is entwined with hers

# November Wind

She crawled out from the nights that twist
and mirror distress

She crawled out of the gloom that
curved for endless miles

She crawled out from the obscurity
and the silence that screamed

Yet her fears disappeared and fell in love
with the November Wind

And she blossomed into something incredible

She crawled out from the slippery connotation
and the nerve-racking innuendos

She crawled out of the heinous remarks
and the bone chilling accusations

She crawled out of the insinuations with daggers
and the lustrous inferences

Yet her anxiety vanished and
 fell in love with the November Wind

And she blossomed into something stunning

She crawled out of the blurred dungeon
and the paraphrases in bold ink

She crawled out of the state of indecision and
the spinning mindset

She crawled out of the nebulous shadow and
and broke away from the chains

Yet her anger melted and
fell in love with the November Wind

And she blossomed into something unbelievable

# Pins and Needles

A very few want to see the colors
I drown myself in
A very few want to see my mascara
run down my alabaster skin
A very few want to love the bits
and fragments of me

In my pins and needles,
I appreciate your gentleness
I appreciate your affection

Love me as much as I adore you

A very few want to see the pages I've written
and read
A very few want to dip their feet
in my creek of agony
A very few want to stay and
hold my tired hands

Love me as much as I cherish you

In my pins and needles
I appreciate your comfort
I appreciate your warmth

A very few want to delve deeper
into the veins of my soul
A very few want to feel my invisible
and burnt scars
A very few want to understand my
sorrow and misfortunes

Love me as much as I savor you

In my pins and needles
I appreciate your grace

# Autumn Kiss

Leaves of aggravation blew away
Leaves of complexity flew away

Leaves of illusions blew away
Leaves of affliction flew away

Your autumn kiss saved my burning soul

Leaves of fragments blew away
Leaves of agony flew away

Leaves of misfortune blew away
Leaves of catastrophe flew away

Your autumn kiss saved my blistering soul

Leaves of emptiness blew away
Leaves of hopelessness flew away

Leaves of heartache blew away
Leaves of solitude flew away

Your autumn kiss saved my smoldering soul

# Dripping Sincerity

I can feel your apology
within your tears of your sincerity
I can feel the threshold
of your tender sincerity

And I fell harder within your vulnerability

I can feel your confession within
your drops of your sincerity
I can feel your compassion
drown in your sincerity

And I fell harder within your vulnerability

I can feel your affection within
the sparkle of your sincerity
I can feel your rainbows twinkling
within your sincerity

And I fell harder within your vulnerability

# Sunset's Flame

When the night falls
I lean in to hear your name
I lean in to feel your distinction

Deep into the sunrise,
I cry for your presence

When the night falls
I lean in to take in your rhapsody
I lean in to gather your pieces

Deep into the sunrise,
I cry for your wisdom

Thank you for being the sunset's flame

When the night falls
I lean in to awaken your shade
I lean in to treasure your ambience

Deep into the sunrise,
I cry for your devotion

When the night falls
I lean in to drown in your scent
I lean in to engrave my dreams

Thank you for being the sunset's flame

# Fly With Me, My Love

I will forever kiss your lost paradigm
I will forever kiss your ballet shoes
I will forever kiss your violin strings

Fly with me, my love

I will forever kiss your sea of hallucinations
I will forever kiss your lucent philosophy
I will forever kiss your complex patterns

Fly with me, my love

I will forever kiss your yearn for knowledge
I will forever kiss your isosceles theories
I will forever kiss your tenacity and hunger

Fly with me, my love

I will forever kiss your abundance of joy
I will forever kiss your lightning and thunder
I will forever kiss your desolate paintings

Fly with me, my love

I will forever kiss your frazzled wings
I will forever kiss your fields of animation
I will forever kiss your candlelit tales

Fly with me, my love

# Two O'clock Bistro

Sapphire eyes shifting to the left
in the Chardonnay air, quietly humming a
melody, slightly neurotic but magnetic,
staring into her sunny side spring salad,
gazing at her soft alabaster skin,

exchanging sarcastic one liner, chuckling
over circus like jokes, stumbling into
a conversation of psychology, the sound of
delicate piano prancing in our ears,
comforting and pleasant, a first date,
surveying her countless layers, probing
her intuition and critical thinking, analytics

spinning in her octagon, appreciation her
fondness of classical music, fumbling into
the intensity of Ayn Rand, dissecting "The
Fountainhead" with an exceptional view,
A beautiful glimpse of the Two O'clock Bistro

# For Me, the Selfish

For me, the selfish
I want all your electrifying skin to myself
Inhaling your mind, cynicism and
charm to dance around your lips
I am on my knees at your wonder
awestruck and guided by your intuition

I am self-indulgent when it comes to your desires
I am self-indulgent when it comes to your wishes

For me, the selfish
I want your affection and castles to breathe
gasping for your dazzling language
entwined with your fluorescent storytelling,
flickering philosophies, off-color dreams
I am hungry for your honey like fascination

I am self-indulgent when it comes to your
candy
I am self-indulgent when it comes to your
insatiable flames

For me, the Selfish,
I want your closeness to transform my edges,
wrapped around my screams soothing me,
admiring your brilliance and path
I am enthusiastic for your excellence
your candor and style consume me

I am self-indulgent when it comes to your mind
I am self-indulgent when it comes to your essence

# Essence

Love me like the sand loves the footprints
Love me like the sky loves the clouds

Love me like the canvas loves the colors
Love me like the trees loves the leaves

I am madly in love with your essence

Love me like the flowers loves the petals
Love me like the earth loves the rain

Love me like the notebook loves the ink
Love me like the eyes loves the tears

I am madly in love with your essence

Love me like the lips loves the kisses
Love me like the lungs loves the air

Love me like the hands loves the touch
Love me like the eyes loves the view

I am madly in love with your essence

Love me like the sky loves the stars
Love me like the ocean loves the fishes

Love me like the skin loves the bones
Love me like the darkness loves the light

I am madly in love with your essence

# At Last, My Valentine

At last, my valentine,
the nightfall is brimming with endearment
whirlwind of emotion, sanctified caress
blossoming affection, flourishing scent
a rapture with a crimson glow
serenity spoken with a delicate accent
kindness spilling from your lips
love is no longer obscure nor a shadow
surrounded by peace, shimmering harmony
desire is not a color of lust, engraved souls
certainty is intertwined, respect is gilded
your halo sparkles and the hurricane fades

# Beside Me

Tomorrow will be
delightful and full of decorated promise
Tomorrow will be
savory with a pinch of generosity

Beside me is a future with you

Tomorrow will be
filled with flavor and dripping moons
Tomorrow will be
effervescent with a splash of tenderness

Beside me is a strong and soft hand

Tomorrow will be
glistening and saturated with peace
Tomorrow will be
blissful with a hint of compassion

Beside me is a never-ending light

# Skin of Courage

I see the beauty in your
mysterious scars and tragedies
I see the beauty in your
self-doubt and inquisitions

And I'm no longer afraid
of your skin of courage

I see the beauty in your
lion like strength and battles
I see the beauty in your
vulnerability and devotion

And I'm no longer afraid
of your skin of courage

I see the beauty in your
wildfire and serene reflections
I see the beauty in your
steel fists and determination

And I'm no longer afraid
of your skin of courage

I see the beauty in your
valiant torch and pale reverence
I see the beauty in your
tears of the untouchable blaze

And I'm no longer afraid
of your skin of courage

# The Gift

Visually she's perfect from head to toe
She has twinkling eyes that shine like diamonds
She has a smile that glows everlasting
She has a fun-loving spirit that should be embraced by all
She has a dynamic style that makes her special
To know her is a gift and a blessing

She has a smell that is intoxicating that I am drowning in
She is a classic and full of vibrating joy
She is a rare breed of women and is simply unique
She has a skin of gold and is priceless jewel
She is sweet brown sugar with a dab of spice
To know her is a gift and a blessing

Visually she is stimulating to the eyes
She has a walk that leaves me catatonic
She has a captivating mind and a gravitating soul
She is the center of what is pure and true
She is a statue of beauty and elegance
God must have taken his time with her
To know her is a gift and a blessing

She is an aphrodisiac and addicting to the eyes
She is a dream come true
She is something you don't find every day
She makes the world go round with her presence
She is amazing and I am in awe
To know her is a gift and a blessing

# Tender and Rare

I could easily fall
for the moon in your twinkling eyes
I could easily fall
for your precious skin

I could easily fall
for your soothing heavenly voice
I could easily fall
for the stars above your head

I could easily fall
for your gentle and warm touch
I could easily fall
for the sweetness on your lips

I could easily fall
for the world held in your palm
I could easily fall
for your charm and wit

I could easily fall
for your enticing sigh
I could easily fall
into your delicate universe

# Colors of Treasure

Love my blackened scars
Love my lopsided flaws
Love my fatal quirks
Love my enigmatic perception

Thank you for loving me

Love my complicated essence
Love my simple comforter
Love my undying will
Love my quivering fears

Thank you for loving me

Love my shadow's tears
Love my effervescent soul
Love my conflicted backbone
Love my distinctive complexion

Thank you for loving me

# MORE BOOKS
## BY BRAEDEN MICHAELS

*The Raven's Poison* a full length collection of poetry characterizing and describing all aspects of the human condition and emotions.

*Stella Walker's Acquaintances* a collection of character poetry surrounding the friends and acquaintances of a widowed woman as she reflects on her life.

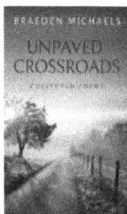

*Unpaved Crossroads* a full length collection of poetry which depicts various scenes and moments in time, with a common theme of specific places throughout.

*Growl from the Sun* a collection of political poetry included Michaels' magnum opus of the same name, opining governmental and civic current events.

*For You, Love Always* a collection of heart-touching and emotionally moving poetry for lovers.

# ABOUT THE AUTHOR

Braeden Michaels is an American author and the creator of Deconstructive Literature. Within the whirlwind of his mind, he gravitates to the darkest edges of humanity and he's here to write about it. He's been featured in a handful of anthologies which include both poetry and a short story. He also has several poetry books published. This is his sixth book.

Braeden's creativity never stops. Constantly observing human nature and analyzing the depths, he continues to write every day. He is currently working on his future collections.

You can read more on his website, braedenmichaels.com.